This recording can be useful to the beginning and the advanced bluegrass guitar player. It contains twelve standard bluegrass songs and two instrumentals with the guitar recorded on one channel and the rest of the instruments on the other. You may tune your guitar to the notes given at the beginning of the record or to any standard tuning device. By adjusting the balance on your stereo you can eliminate the guitar and then play along as the group's guitarist. Or, you can isolate the guitar playing and listen to it more carefully.

For the beginner, this book contains the chords to all the songs and some basic instruction on rhythm guitar playing. It enables you to play along with the record at your own level.

Instruction is also offered in more sophisticated back-up playing, including many of the bass runs heard on the album. The guitar breaks or solos on the record range from the fairly simple (Jesse James, Late Last Night, and Little Maggie) to the very difficult (Foggy Mountain Breakdown, It's In My Mind To Ramble).

Tablature, a form of musical notation, is included for all the breaks. The more advanced player may learn the breaks from the tablature and play them along with the record. When working with tablature it is extremely important to listen to the music to hear how it should sound. Feel free also to make up your own solos and try them out with the band.

HOW TO READ TABLATURE AND MUSIC

In guitar tablature the six lines represent the six strings of the guitar, with the bass E as the bottom line.

The numbers on the lines indicate which fret is being fingered on a particular string. So, a G chord is represented as:

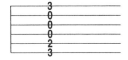

Rhythmic values of notes are indicated as in regular written music. Most of the tunes on the record are in $\frac{2}{4}$ time. This means there are two beats (quarter notes) per measure. $\frac{4}{4}$ time has four beats and $\frac{3}{4}$ time three beats per measure. Each quarter note can be divided evenly into two eighth notes or four sixteenth notes. An eighth note lasts half as

long as a quarter note, and a sixteenth note lasts half as long as an eighth note. Thus, for every tap of the foot in Roll On Buddy there are four sixteenth notes or two eighth notes.

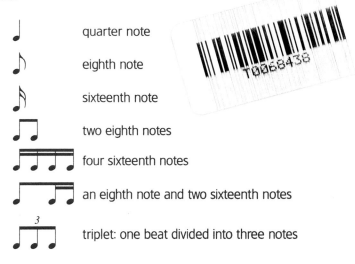

When two of the same notes are connected by a ⌒ their rhythmic values are added together to make a longer note. If a note is followed by a dot it is held one and one-half times as long as usual. Thus:

$$ ♪. = ♪ \smile ♪ \qquad\qquad ♩. = ♩ \smile ♪ $$

𝄾   indicates a rest or pause for the duration of one quarter note

𝄾   indicates a rest for the duration of one eighth note.

𝄾   indicates a rest for the duration of one sixteenth note.

—   indicates a rest for two beats.

—   indicates a rest for four beats.

If you keep your foot tapping and listen to the music on the record constantly as you learn, you should not have any trouble reading the notation. If you are still confused about it, however, it would be helpful to consult a music text to clarify the reading and counting of rhythmic notation.

Two notes tied together with the letter "H" above indicates a "hammer-on". A "P" indicates a "pull-off". An "S" indicates a slide from one fret to another. All are means by which the left hand causes a note to sound.

⊓   indicates a downstroke of the pick.

V   indicates an upstroke of the pick.

These symbols are found above the line of tablature being read.

MMO CD 3608

CHORD CHART

These are the basic chords used in the songs on the recording, (numbers show left hand fingering):

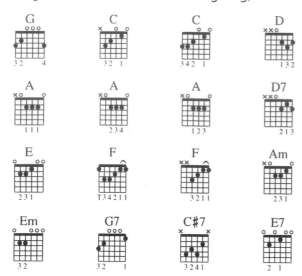

PLAYING BACKUP

When you play bluegrass rhythm guitar, hold the flatpick securely between your thumb and the side of the last segment of your index finger, but don't squeeze so tightly that you cramp your hand. The basic musical pattern consists of a bass note followed by a strum of the chord, followed by a bass note, then a strum, etc. For example, in a G chord:

sounds like "boom chink"

There are two alternatives to the single strum shown above. One is the double strum, consisting of one strum down followed quickly by another one up with the pick. The other pattern involves a triple strum. Both are shown below left:

sounds like "boom chinka"

sounds like "boompa chinka"

To simplify notation the bass notes are written as eighth or sixteenth notes. They should, however, ring for an entire beat. Don't worry too much about hitting the exact number of strings indicated on the strums. Just strive for a smooth sound. The type of strumming pattern you use depends on the tempo and general feel of a song. Use your judgement to decide which pattern sounds best on a particular song, and feel free to combine strums within a measure. For example:

I would recommend using a heavy flatpick. It may feel awkward at first, but it will eventually enable you to get the best sound with the surest control. Try to remain loose at the wrist and elbow as you play. There should be some movement at both joints. Try to maintain a solid beat, an even rhythm, and a full sound. To compete with a banjo, fiddle, and a mandolin you cannot afford to play too softly, so hit the strings with a fairly firm stroke. Be patient. It takes some time and practice to be able to combine speed, clarity, and volume in your playing.

The following music and tablature shows you what bass notes to play in the strumming patterns for most chords commonly found in bluegrass.

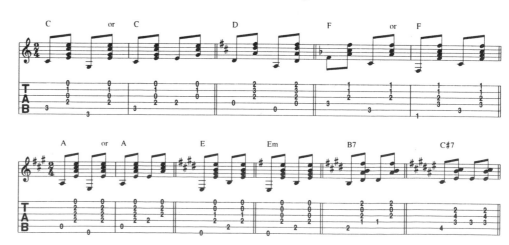

DARK HOLLOW

Here is an example of simple back-up for a chorus of "Dark Hollow."

Capo II, sounds in Key of E

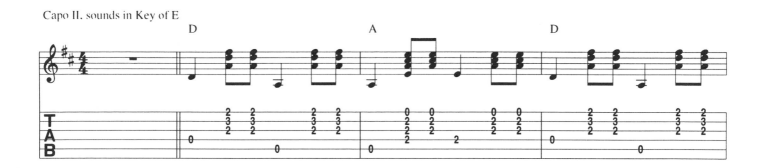

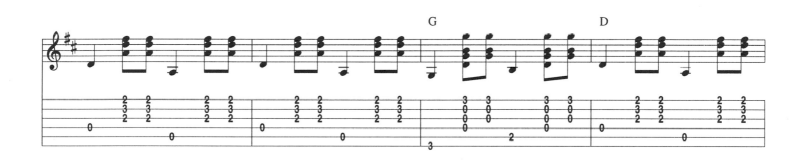

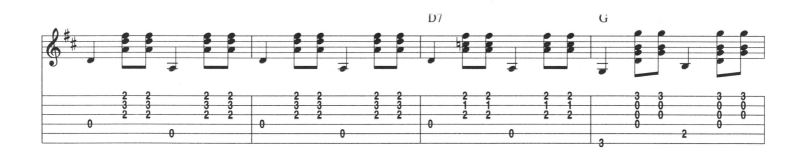

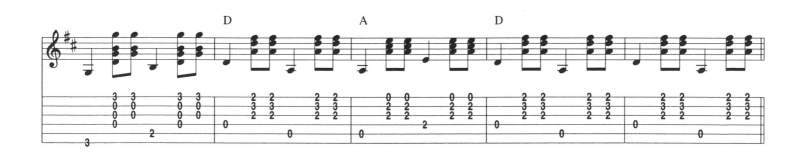

MMO CD 3608

ROLL ON BUDDY

Bass runs within a chord and from one chord to another make playing more interesting and add movement to the music. Included below for some of the songs is tablature for a representative segment of rhythm guitar playing as heard on the recording. These examples should give you a feel for using runs in your back-up playing.

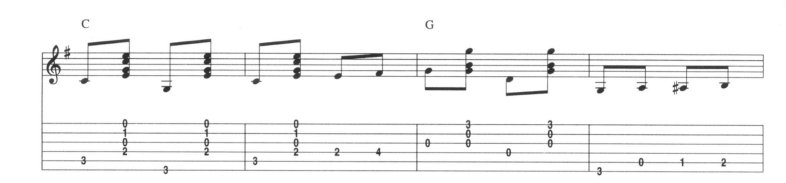

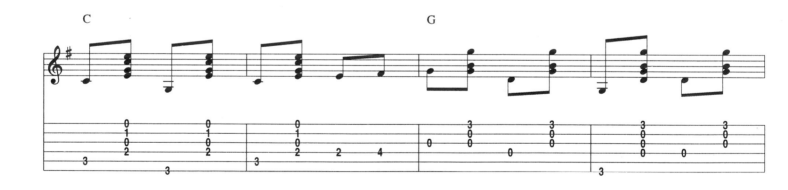

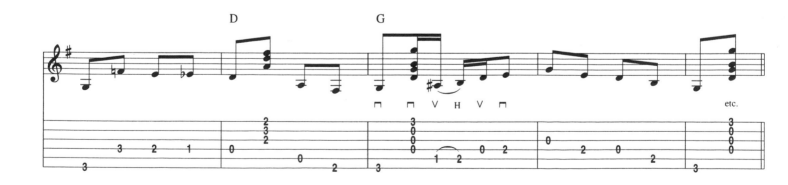

ALL THE GOOD TIMES ARE PAST AND GONE

Capo IV, sounds in Key of B (Back-up heard behind opening fiddle break)

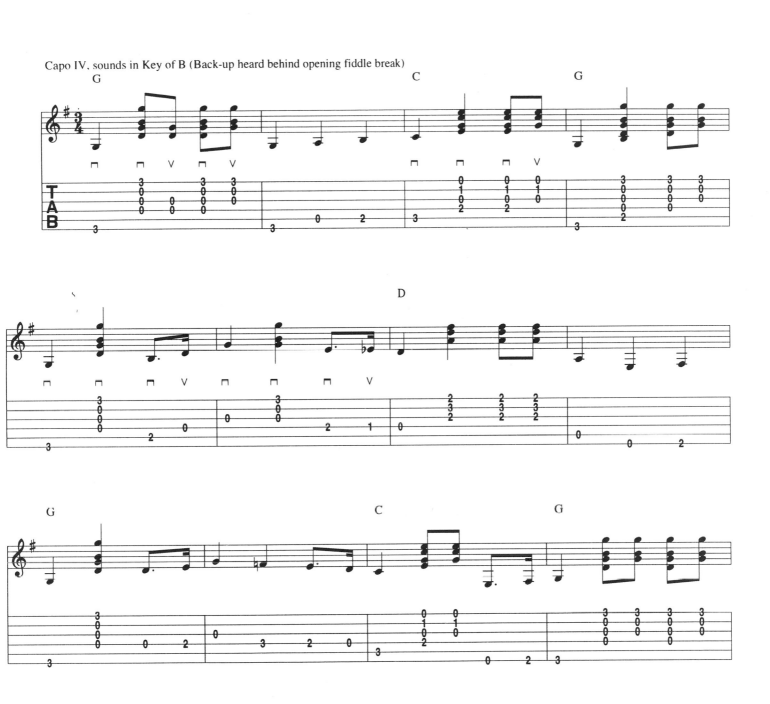

MMO CD 3608

LATE LAST NIGHT

Capo II, sounds in Key of A (Back-up heard behind first verse)

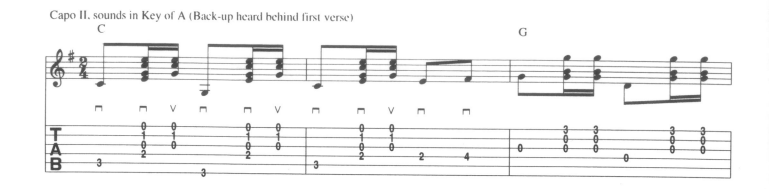

LONESOME ROAD BLUES

Capo II, sounds in Key of B, use either single or double strum (Heard behind first chorus.)

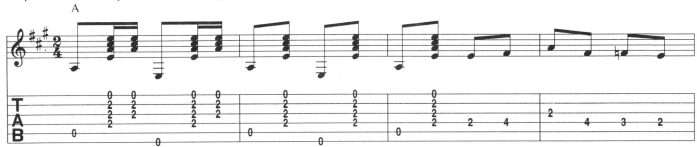

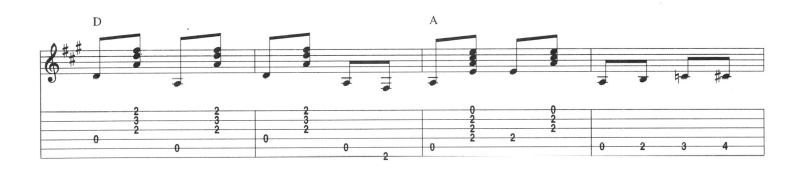

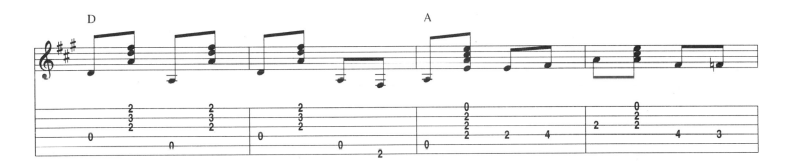

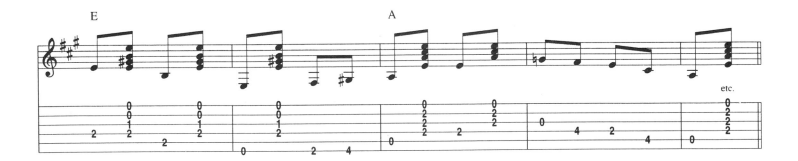

9

THE BALLAD OF JED CLAMPETT

BY PAUL HENNING

Opening count: 1 2 3 4, 1 2 3. No guitar break.

Sounds in Key of G.

> G   Am   D   G
> Come and listen to my story 'bout a man named Jed, a poor mountaineer, barely kept his family fed
>
>   C   C♯7   D   G
> And then one day he was shootin' at some food, up from the ground come a bubblin' crude.

FOGGY MOUNTAIN BREAKDOWN

BY EARL SCRUGGS

Opening count: 1 2 3 4, 1 2 3. There are 11 choruses. The guitar plays this break for the eighth and ninth choruses (after second banjo break).

Key of G

*This is a very quick hammer-on from fret 2 to 3 on the second string as the first string, first fret is struck simultaneously with the pick.

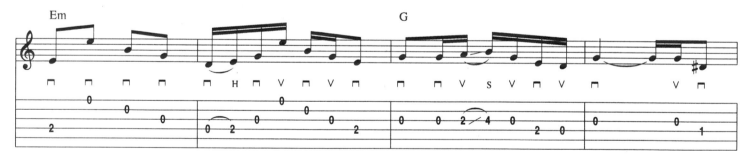

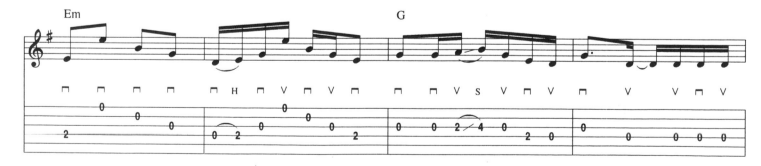

beginning of second time through

11

It's In My Mind To Ramble

by Peter Wernick

Opening count: 1 2 3. Guitar takes third break.

	G		F		G	
Verse:	It's been quite a while since I've seen you my dear. I've been gone a long, long time.			D	G	

	F	G	D	G
All those nights on the road I've been talking to myself, I can't believe I left you behind.

	G		F	G
Chorus:	It's in my mind to ramble. I hope you'll understand. Sometimes I find I just have to go.

	C	G	D	G
I know it's hard my darling, forgive me if you can 'cause you know that I love you so.

SALTY DOG BLUES

Opening count: 1 2 3. Guitar takes third break.

Capo II, sounding key of A

G   **E**

Standing on the corner with the low down blues

   A

A great big hole in the bottom of my shoes

D   **G**

Honey let me be your salty dog. (*chords repeat*)

MMO CD 3608

DARK HOLLOW

Opening count: 1 2 3. Guitar takes second break.

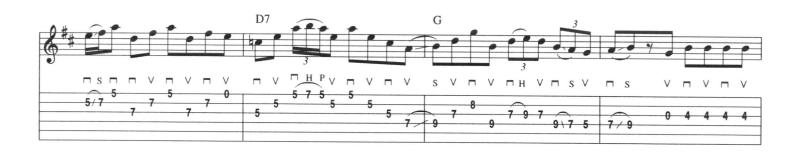

    D **A**   **D**   **G**   **D**

I'd rather be in some dark hollow where the sun refuse to shine

             D7 **G**   **D**   **A**   **D**

Than to be here alone, knowin' that you're gone, it would cause me to lose my mind.

LATE LAST NIGHT

Opening count: 1 2 3. Guitar takes second break.

Capo II, sounding Key of A

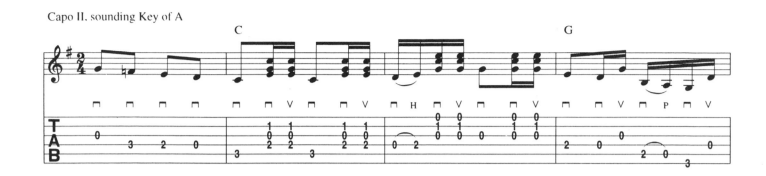

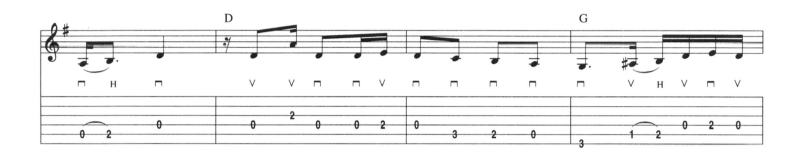

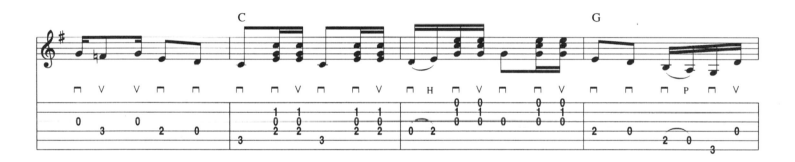

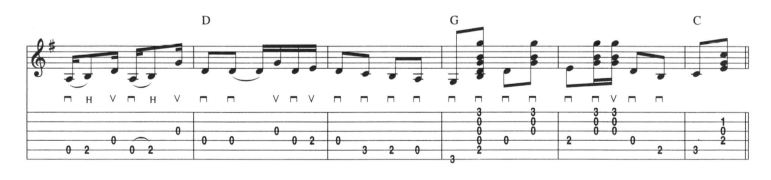

C	G	D	G

It was late last night when Willie came home, heard him a rappin' on the door.

C	G	D	G

Slippin' and a slidin' with them new shoes on, Papa said, "Willie, don't you rap no more."

MMO CD 3608

DUELING BANJOS

Opening count: 1 2 3 4. This is the first half of the arrangement on the record.

Track 9, 23

MOUNTAIN DEW

Opening count: 1 2, 1 2. Guitar takes opening break.

Capo II. sounding Key of A

*Indicates a very quick slide in which the duration of the note on the second fret is almost negligible.

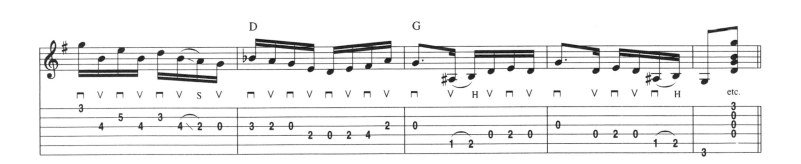

    G   C   G

Now my Uncle Mort, he's sawed off and short. He measures 'bout four foot two.

                                                   D   G

But he thinks he's a giant when they give him a pint of that good old mountain dew.

17

MMO CD 3608

LONESOME ROAD BLUES

Opening count: 1 2 3 4, 1 2 3. No guitar break.

Capo II. Sounds in Key of B. Opening count: 1 2 3 4, 1 2 3.

A   D   A

I'm going down that long lonesome road, Lord, Lord. I'm going down that long lonesome road

D   A   E   A

Going down that lone lonesome road Lord, Lord, and I ain't gonna be treated this a way.

LITTLE MAGGIE

A   G   A   E   A

Oh, yonder stand little Maggie with a dram glass in her hand

         G   A   E   A

She's drinking away her troubles and courting another man.

ALL THE GOOD TIMES ARE PAST AND GONE

Opening count: 1 2 3, 1. Guitar takes second break.

Capo IV, sounding Key of B

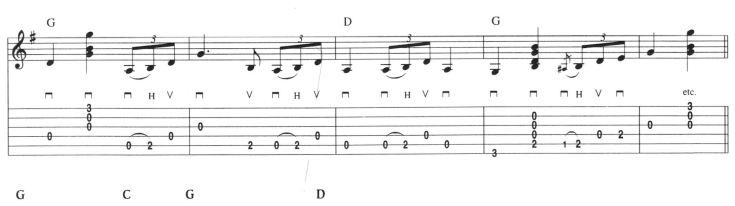

G   **C**   **G**   **D**

I wish to the Lord I'd never been born or died when I was young

G   **C**   **G**   **D** **G**

I never wuold have seen your sparkling blue eyes or heard your lying tongue.

MMO CD 3608

ROLL ON BUDDY

Opening count: 1 2 3. Guitar takes third break.

Capo IV, sounding Key of B

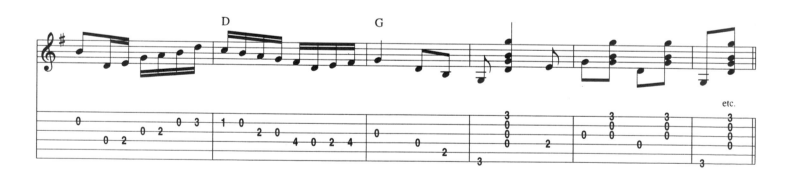

G   C   G

I'm going to that east pay road. I'm going to the east pay road.

C   G   D   G

I'm going to the east, I'm going to the west, I'm going to the one that I love best.

SITTING ON TOP OF THE WORLD

Opening count: 1 2 3 4, 1 2 3. Guitar takes fourth break.

Capo V, sounding Key of C

G   **C**   **G**

Was in the spring, one sunny day, my good gal left me, Lord, she went away.

                                                           D   **G**

And now she's gone, and I don't worry, 'cause I'm sitting on top of the world.

MMO CD 3608

JESSE JAMES

Opening count: 1 2 3. Guitar takes second break.

Key of C

Verse:

C		F	C		G	

Jesse James was a lad who killed many a man. He robbed the Glendale train.

C		F	C	G		C

He stole from the rich and he gave to the poor with a hand, a heart, and a brain.

Chorus:

F		C		G	

Jesse had a wife to mourn for his life, three children, they were brave.

C		F	C	G		C

But that dirty little coward that shot Mr. Howard, has laid poor Jesse in his grave.

MMO Compact Disc Catalog

BROADWAY

LES MISERABLES/PHANTOM OF THE OPERA	MMO CD 1016
HITS OF ANDREW LLOYD WEBBER	MMO CD 1054
GUYS AND DOLLS	MMO CD 1067
WEST SIDE STORY 2 CD Set	MMO CD 1100
CABARET 2 CD Set	MMO CD 1110
BROADWAY HEROES AND HEROINES	MMO CD 1121
CAMELOT	MMO CD 1173
BEST OF ANDREW LLOYD WEBBER	MMO CD 1130
THE SOUND OF BROADWAY	MMO CD 1133
BROADWAY MELODIES	MMO CD 1134
BARBRA'S BROADWAY	MMO CD 1144
JEKYLL & HYDE	MMO CD 1151
SHOWBOAT	MMO CD 1160
MY FAIR LADY 2 CD Set	MMO CD 1174
OKLAHOMA!	MMO CD 1175
THE SOUND OF MUSIC 2 CD Set	MMO CD 1176
SOUTH PACIFIC	MMO CD 1177
THE KING AND I	MMO CD 1178
FIDDLER ON THE ROOF 2 CD Set	MMO CD 1179
CAROUSEL	MMO CD 1180
PORGY AND BESS	MMO CD 1181
THE MUSIC MAN	MMO CD 1183
ANNIE GET YOUR GUN 2 CD Set	MMO CD 1186
HELLO DOLLY! 2 CD Set	MMO CD 1187
OLIVER 2 CD Set	MMO CD 1189
SUNSET BOULEVARD	MMO CD 1193
GREASE	MMO CD 1196
SMOKEY JOE'S CAFE	MMO CD 1197

CLARINET

MOZART CONCERTO, IN A	MMO CD 3201
WEBER CONCERTO NO. 1 IN FM. STAMITZ CON. NO. 3 IN BB	MMO CD 3202
SPOHR CONCERTO NO. 1 IN C MINOR OP. 26	MMO CD 3203
WEBER CONCERTO OP. 26, BEETHOVEN TRIO OP. 11	MMO CD 3204
FIRST CHAIR CLARINET SOLOS	MMO CD 3205
THE ART OF THE SOLO CLARINET	MMO CD 3206
MOZART QUINTET IN A, K.581	MMO CD 3207
BRAHMS SONATAS OP. 120 NO. 1 & 2	MMO CD 3208
WEBER GRAND DUO CONCERTANT WAGNER ADAGIO	MMO CD 3209
SCHUMANN FANTASY OP. 73, 3 ROMANCES OP. 94	MMO CD 3210
EASY CLARINET SOLOS Volume 1 - STUDENT LEVEL	MMO CD 3211
EASY CLARINET SOLOS Volume 2 - STUDENT LEVEL	MMO CD 3212
EASY JAZZ DUETS - STUDENT LEVEL	MMO CD 3213
BEGINNING CONTEST SOLOS - Jerome Bunke, Clinician	MMO CD 3221
BEGINNING CONTEST SOLOS - Harold Wright	MMO CD 3222
INTERMEDIATE CONTEST SOLOS - Stanley Drucker	MMO CD 3223
INTERMEDIATE CONTEST SOLOS - Jerome Bunke, Clinician	MMO CD 3224
ADVANCED CONTEST SOLOS - Stanley Drucker	MMO CD 3225
ADVANCED CONTEST SOLOS - Harold Wright	MMO CD 3226
INTERMEDIATE CONTEST SOLOS - Stanley Drucker	MMO CD 3227
ADVANCED CONTEST SOLOS - Stanley Drucker	MMO CD 3228
ADVANCED CONTEST SOLOS - Harold Wright	MMO CD 3229

PIANO

BEETHOVEN CONCERTO NO 1 IN C	MMO CD 3001
BEETHOVEN CONCERTO NO. 2 IN Bb	MMO CD 3002
BEETHOVEN CONCERTO NO. 3 IN C MINOR	MMO CD 3003
BEETHOVEN CONCERTO NO. 4 IN G	MMO CD 3004
BEETHOVEN CONCERTO NO. 5 IN Eb (2 CD SET)	MMO CD 3005
GRIEG CONCERTO IN A MINOR OP.16	MMO CD 3006
RACHMANINOFF CONCERTO NO. 2 IN C MINOR	MMO CD 3007
SCHUMANN CONCERTO IN A MINOR	MMO CD 3008
BRAHMS CONCERTO NO. 1 IN D MINOR (2 CD SET)	MMO CD 3009
CHOPIN CONCERTO NO. 1 IN E MINOR OP. 11	MMO CD 3010
MENDELSSOHN CONCERTO NO. 1 IN G MINOR	MMO CD 3011
MOZART CONCERTO NO. 9 IN Eb K.271	MMO CD 3012
MOZART CONCERTO NO. 12 IN A K.414	MMO CD 3013
MOZART CONCERTO NO. 20 IN D MINOR K.466	MMO CD 3014
MOZART CONCERTO NO. 23 IN A K.488	MMO CD 3015
MOZART CONCERTO NO. 24 IN C MINOR K.491	MMO CD 3016
MOZART CONCERTO NO. 26 IN D K.537, CORONATION	MMO CD 3017
MOZART CONCERTO NO. 17 IN G K.453	MMO CD 3018
LISZT CONCERTO NO. 1 IN Eb, WEBER OP. 79	MMO CD 3019
LISZT CONCERTO NO. 2 IN A, HUNGARIAN FANTASIA	MMO CD 3020
J.S. BACH CONCERTO IN F MINOR, J.C. BACH CON. IN Eb	MMO CD 3021
J.S. BACH CONCERTO IN D MINOR	MMO CD 3022
HAYDN CONCERTO IN D	MMO CD 3023
HEART OF THE PIANO CONCERTO	MMO CD 3024
THEMES FROM GREAT PIANO CONCERTI	MMO CD 3025
TSCHAIKOVSKY CONCERTO NO. 1 IN Bb MINOR	MMO CD 3026
ART OF POPULAR PIANO PLAYING, Vol. 1 STUDENT LEVEL	MMO CD 3033
ART OF POPULAR PIANO PLAYING, Vol. 2 STUDENT LEVEL 2 CD Set	MMO CD 3034
'POP' PIANO FOR STARTERS STUDENT LEVEL	MMO CD 3035
MOZART COMPLETE MUSIC FOR PIANO FOUR HANDS 2 CD Set	MMO CD 3036

INSTRUCTIONAL METHODS

RUTGERS UNIVERSITY MUSIC DICTATION/EAR TRAINING COURSE (7 CD Set)	MMO CD 7001
EVOLUTION OF THE BLUES	MMO CD 7004
THE ART OF IMPROVISATION, VOL. 1	MMO CD 7005
THE ART OF IMPROVISATION, VOL. 2	MMO CD 7006
THE BLUES MINUS YOU Ed Xiques, Soloist	MMO CD 7007

VIOLIN

BRUCH CONCERTO NO. 1 IN G MINOR OP.26	MMO CD 3100
MENDELSSOHN CONCERTO IN E MINOR	MMO CD 3101
TSCHAIKOVSKY CONCERTO IN D OP. 35	MMO CD 3102
BACH DOUBLE CONCERTO IN D MINOR	MMO CD 3103
BACH CONCERTO IN A MINOR, CONCERTO IN E	MMO CD 3104
BACH BRANDENBURG CONCERTI NOS. 4 & 5	MMO CD 3105
BACH BRANDENBURG CONCERTO NO. 2, TRIPLE CONCERTO	MMO CD 3106
BACH CONCERTO IN DM, (FROM CONCERTO FOR HARPSICHORD)	MMO CD 3107
BRAHMS CONCERTO IN D OP. 77	MMO CD 3108
CHAUSSON POEME, SCHUBERT RONDO	MMO CD 3109
LALO SYMPHONIE ESPAGNOLE	MMO CD 3110
MOZART CONCERTO IN D K.218, VIVALDI CON. AM OP.3 NO.6	MMO CD 3111
MOZART CONCERTO IN A K.219	MMO CD 3112
WIENIAWSKI CON. IN D. SARASATE ZIGEUNERWEISEN	MMO CD 3113
VIOTTI CONCERTO NO.22	MMO CD 3114
BEETHOVEN 2 ROMANCES, SONATA NO. 5 IN F "SPRING SONATA"	MMO CD 3115
SAINT-SAENS INTRODUCTION & RONDO,	
MOZART SERENADE K. 204, ADAGIO K.261	MMO CD 3116
BEETHOVEN CONCERTO IN D OP. 61(2 CD SET)	MMO CD 3117
THE CONCERTMASTER	MMO CD 3118
AIR ON A G STRING Favorite Encores with Orchestra Easy Medium	MMO CD 3119
CONCERT PIECES FOR THE SERIOUS VIOLINIST Easy Medium	MMO CD 3120
18TH CENTURY VIOLIN PIECES	MMO CD 3121
ORCHESTRAL FAVORITES - Volume 1 - Easy Level	MMO CD 3122
ORCHESTRAL FAVORITES - Volume 2 - Medium Level	MMO CD 3123
ORCHESTRAL FAVORITES - Volume 3 - Med to Difficult Level	MMO CD 3124
THE THREE B'S BACH/BEETHOVEN/BRAHMS	MMO CD 3125
VIVALDI Concerto in A Minor Op. 3 No. 6. in D Op. 3 No. 9.	
Double Concerto Op. 3 No. 8	MMO CD 3126
VIVALDI-THE FOUR SEASONS (2 CD Set)	MMO CD 3127
VIVALDI Concerto in Eb, Op. 8, No. 5. ALBINONI Concerto in A	MMO CD 3128
VIVALDI Concerto in E, Op. 3, No. 12. Concerto in C Op. 8, No. 6 "Il Piacere"	MMO CD 3129
SCHUBERT Three Sonatinas	MMO CD 3130
HAYDN String Quartet Op. 76 No. 1	MMO CD 3131
HAYDN String Quartet Op. 76 No. 2	MMO CD 3132
HAYDN String Quartet Op. 76 No. 3 "Emperor"	MMO CD 3133
HAYDN String Quartet Op. 76 No. 4 "Sunrise"	MMO CD 3134
HAYDN String Quartet Op. 76 No. 5	MMO CD 3135
HAYDN String Quartet Op. 76 No. 6	MMO CD 3136
BEAUTIFUL MUSIC FOR TWO VIOLINS 1st position, vol. 1	MMO CD 3137
BEAUTIFUL MUSIC FOR TWO VIOLINS 2nd position, vol. 2	MMO CD 3138
BEAUTIFUL MUSIC FOR TWO VIOLINS 3rd position, vol. 3	MMO CD 3139
BEAUTIFUL MUSIC FOR TWO VIOLINS 1st, 2nd, 3rd position, vol. 4	MMO CD 3140
BARTOK: 44 DUETS	MMO CD 3141

Lovely folk tunes and selections from the classics, chosen for their melodic beauty and technical value. They have been skillfully transcribed and edited by Samuel Applebaum, one of America's foremost teachers.

CELLO

DVORAK Concerto in B Minor Op. 104 (2 CD Set)	MMO CD 3701
C.P.E. BACH Concerto in A Minor	MMO CD 3702
BOCCHERINI Concerto in Bb, BRUCH Kol Nidrei	MMO CD 3703
TEN PIECES FOR CELLO	MMO CD 3704
SCHUMANN Concerto in Am & Other Selections	MMO CD 3705
CLAUDE BOLLING Suite For Cello & Jazz Piano Trio	MMO CD 3706

OBOE

ALBINONI Concerti in Bb, Op. 7 No. 3, No. 6, Dm Op. 9 No. 2	MMO CD 3400
TELEMANN Conc. in Fm; HANDEL Conc. in Bb; VIVALDI Conc.in Dm	MMO CD 3401
MOZART Quartet in F K.370, STAMITZ Quartet in F Op. 8 No. 3	MMO CD 3402
BACH Brandenburg Concerto No. 2, Telemann Con. in Am	MMO CD 3403
CLASSIC SOLOS FOR OBOE Delia Montenegro, Soloist	MMO CD 3404

GUITAR

BOCCHERINI Quintet No. 4 in D "Fandango"	MMO CD 3601
GIULIANI Quintet in A Op. 65	MMO CD 3602
CLASSICAL GUITAR DUETS	MMO CD 3603
RENAISSANCE & BAROQUE GUITAR DUETS	MMO CD 3604
CLASSICAL & ROMANTIC GUITAR DUETS	MMO CD 3605
GUITAR AND FLUTE DUETS Volume 1	MMO CD 3606
GUITAR AND FLUTE DUETS Volume 2	MMO CD 3607
BLUEGRASS GUITAR CLASSIC PIECES minus you	MMO CD 3608
GEORGE BARNES GUITAR METHOD Lessons from a Master	MMO CD 3609
HOW TO PLAY FOLK GUITAR 2 CD Set	MMO CD 3610
FAVORITE FOLKS SONGS FOR GUITAR	MMO CD 3611
FOR GUITARS ONLY! Jimmy Raney Small Band Arrangements	MMO CD 3612
TEN DUETS FOR TWO GUITARS Geo. Barnes/Carl Kress	MMO CD 3613
PLAY THE BLUES GUITAR A Dick Weissman Method	MMO CD 3614
ORCHESTRAL GEMS FOR CLASSICAL GUITAR	MMO CD 3615

BANJO

BLUEGRASS BANJO Classic & Favorite Banjo Pieces	MMO CD 4401
PLAY THE FIVE STRING BANJO Vol. 1 Dick Weissman Method	MMO CD 4402
PLAY THE FIVE STRING BANJO Vol. 2 Dick Weissman Method	MMO CD 4403

FLUTE

MOZART Concerto No. 2 in D, QUANTZ Concerto in G	MMO CD 3300
MOZART Concerto in G K.313	MMO CD 3301
BACH Suite No. 2 in B Minor	MMO CD 3302

MMO Compact Disc Catalog